MW01006953

"Formed by desire, feminin
trauma," Gwen Benaway's sophomore poetry collection is
an astounding, expansive pool of fresh water in Canadian
literature. As she undulates, she blurs the lines between the
body of the poet and the reader, inviting us through *Passage*,
to reflect, cleanse, drown and surface a-new."

—Vivek Shraya, author of *She of the Mountains*
and *even this page is white*

■ ■ ■

"The poet knows how to remember time and place like no
other. In this tradition, Gwen Benaway remembers and
writes about time and place with devoted and delicate
precision. But Benaway does more than reveal time and
place. She allows temporal memory to witness her in return.
With reverence and with reciprocity, she shows how the
land has shaped her body, spirit and identity. These poems
are a conversation between the poet and lake, sky, trees and
earth; a call and response between memory and future
healing, future possibility. These poems are a remarkably-
crafted communication that invites the reader into an
immersive knowledge. *Passage* is a gift of Gwen Benaway's
hard-earned wisdom. Readers, let us say thank you."

—Amber Dawn, author of
How Poetry Saved My Life: A Hustler's Memoir

"There are poets who write about the world's delicate beauty; there are poets who indict the world's terrible cruelty. And there are those fierce and formidable poets like Gwen Benaway who dance that narrow ledge between anguish and awakening, whose searing work leaves you shaken, your heart opened wide in raw and unexpected, welcome grace. *Passage* is a book we've needed for so long: courageous, compassionate, and relentlessly honest about the price of living one's full truth—and the beauty in that possibility. Benaway is a powerful voice in the emerging generation of Indigenous writers who are transforming our all-too-simplistic expectations of identity, embodiment, and kinship, in all the very best ways."

—Daniel Heath Justice (Cherokee Nation),
Canada Research Chair in Indigenous Literature and
Expressive Culture, University of British Columbia

■ ■ ■

PASSAGE

PASSAGE

Gwen Benaway

Published By Kegedonce Press
11 Park Road, Neyaashiinigmiing, Ontario N0H 2T0 www.kegedonce.com
Administration Office/Book Orders: P.O. Box 517, Owen Sound, ON N4K 5R1

Sales: mandagroup.com, Distribution: litdistco.ca,
Customer Service/orders: Tel 1-800-591-6250 / Fax 1-800-591-6251 / orders@litdistco.ca
LitDistCo c/o Fraser Direct, 8300 Lawson Rd., Milton ON L9T 0A4

Passage
ISBN 978-1-928120-08-7

We acknowledge the support of the Canada Council for the Arts, which last year invested $153 million to bring the arts to Canadians throughout the country.
Nous remercions le Conseil des arts du Canada de son soutien. L'an dernier, le Conseil a investi 153 millions de dollars pour mettre de l'art dans la vie des Canadiennes et des Canadiens de tout le pays.

Canada Council Conseil des arts
for the Arts   du Canada

The publisher gratefully acknowledges the support of
The Ontario Arts Council for its publishing program.

ONTARIO ARTS COUNCIL
CONSEIL DES ARTS DE L'ONTARIO
an Ontario government agency
un organisme du gouvernement de l'Ontario

Front Cover image: Susan Blight (artist from Couchiching First Nation)
Text Design and Print Production, Beth Crane, WeMakeBooks.ca

4th printing, July 2018

Printed in Canada

"I've trust enough in all
that's happened in my life,
the unexpected love
and gentleness that rushes in
to fill the arid spaces
in my heart, the way the city
glow fills up the sky
above the river, making it
seem less than night."
—Tim Dlugos, "G-9"
from *A Fast Life: The Collected Poems of Tim Dlugos* (1982)

"So it is better to speak
remembering
we were never meant to survive."
—Audre Lorde, "A Litany For Survival",
The Black Unicorn: Poems (1995)

"Burning up myself, I would leave fire behind me."
—Robin Blaser, *The Fire* (1967)

"When a woman tells the truth she is creating
the possibility for more truth around her."
—Adrienne Rich, "*Women and Honor:
Some Notes on Lying*," 191 (1977)

Dedicated to the girls like me.
You know who you are.

Contents

Lake Michigan

Lake Huron

Lake Ontario

Lake Erie

Lake Superior

LAKE MICHIGAN

Lake Michigan

when the question
has no easy answer,
I weave a second life
to please the curious.

where are you from
is do you belong,
who claims you
in softer words.

I answer here,
this land between
countries and water,
the Great Lakes,

where my ancestors
grew and died
along the shoreline
of every waterway.

not a whole truth
but true enough
to cross the threshold
of memorial.

we began in you,
blue light holds us
in your sunken veins,
Lake Michigan

in your split bones
before the army
and the Jesuits
invaded like frost.

from your marrow
we grew, mixed seeds
with a single promise,
not a new nation

but an old gift,
memory of life
before quantum,
racial accounting.

they trace us
back into origin,
by church records
and county registers,

it's your body
they should map,
arteries of trade
with no ill tide

when they ask,
at a poetry reading
or a second date,
I'll not deny you.

name you home,
the undercurrent
in the cold dark,
Lake Michigan's lodge

bed of my ancestors,
shale lined dreams
spirits of yellow perch
navigate tributaries of us,

a swell rises up to light
before it disappears,
breaking but never bound,
our history dissolves

when they try to fathom it.

North Shore

I build walls,
the land carries me over them.
on the other side, water waits.

through the inner country,
tributaries, the bay's curve;
I go out to drown.

captive to current,
no one here to portage,
I leave my body behind.

ancestral home, the Great Lakes
and the muskeg past them, boreal
veins of where the dead camp.

they built nothing, just etchings
and a midden heap of shells.
interpretation centres trail the highway.

I follow them to Thunder Bay,
I ask to be clean of everything,
reconnected, plugged in.

It's not about escape,
but yes, I left town.
who am I now?

I won't call anyone,
there's no one left, just wind,
the sound of geese flying.

when I push past borders,
hiding in a Northern truck stop,
I find no road maps.

just the memory of the dead,
echoes of a people and a place
I only name in translation.

outward bound isn't healing,
north of Sudbury, I owe up–
I wasn't in love.

the wilderness knows me better,
I find shelter in the canopy
of pine, loose stones.

I don't regret love,
but why did it take me
so long to leave

and find another life,
along the North Shore,
where my heart grows

big by Lake Superior,
deep rooted, mud cast,
in the mouths of my dead.

Willows

in every swamp,
there is a breaking point,
too much moisture
under the skin.

you would never know
where the water lies
so deep in the soil
that it sinks down.

the surface looks the same
as the rest of the swamp,
ferns, mottled red leaves,
and the smell of decay.

but if you step there,
by mistake or design,
you will be pulled through
to the swamp's underbelly.

your feet captured,
legs sucked down
while you tip forward
into the slow descent.

there is no solid ground
at the breaking point,
no easy escape anywhere,
just gravity and silt.

I found this out
the hard way,
a teenager alone
in the backcountry.

I pulled free, up and out
using a strand of willows,
their long roots enough
to bear the whole of me.

I swore it was the last time
I would cross the swamp's borders
but then I met you–all bets off–
look where it's brought me.

the dusk of early autumn,
these wet boots, a handful of mud,
your weight on my shoulders,
and no willows in sight.

Addict

by the lake with a morning cigarette,
I thank the ancestors for nothing.

I bring up their long absence,
the silence that rattles in me.

I let my exhales rise up,
blackened lungs deflating.

I butt out before they answer,
tired of the same replies.

if longing for the dead is a craving,
then smoking is a kind of remedy.

answer the past with its proxy,
white smoke and the aftertaste

of metal and ashes.

If

if night comes,
if the stars align,
if spirits walk North,
if the ghosts are kind,
I'll find a safe inlet.

if I make camp,
if driftwood fire catches,
if dawn hovers in the eastern sky,
if the morning birds stay hushed,
I can sleep tonight.

if the weather changes,
if my coat is warm enough,
if the wool lining dries in time,
if the rain holds off till noon,
I might stay alive.

if I survive this stupid quest,
if ancestral memory is enough,
if this halfbreed doesn't disappear,
if I meet my ride at the pickup point,
I can say I did it.

if the paper map is right,
if our land is really a mother,
if there isn't an angry bear,
if my elders aren't full of shit,
I might be 5 miles from home.

if I forget the boy,
if all the boys forget me,
if I murder desire on the Northern Shield,
if a granite sky unmakes me under nimbus clouds,
I may undo history-everyone's history.

if exploration isn't always conquest,
if discovery can be shaped of visions,
if instinct is another word for truth,
if passage is more than movement,
I've already made it back.

Kiiwe

I miss my gookum's farmhouse,
the only safe place of childhood.

It wasn't happy but violence had to wait,
on pause till the aunties left,

here I learned to love the unspoken,
a life of secondhand smoke and black tea.

sitting at the kitchen table, piled in nutri-sweet,
their torn pink wrappers hiding the tablecloth,

my uncle and father in their worn out armchairs,
holes in the backing like the pauses in their voices,

mice and the garter snakes in the front porch,
hiding behind a freezer of discount ice cream

Michigan woods circling us, a dividing line
between the house and dirt roads to nowhere.

I can't go back now, she died,
a ghost among ghosts in a dead family,

two sets of grandparents, my favourite uncle
and the aunt who raised horses, my cousin at 21.

the waiting dead pile up, my mother
as she shrinks to calcium, becomes elemental.

I haven't heard my father's voice in 4 years,
he won't shake my boyfriend's hand.

still memory stays alive, flickers down
the highway and travels through bones,

I want them back even if they escape me,
even if they've soured in death and absence.

going home- *kiiwe*- is a verb I can't get rid of,
because it translates to loss in every tongue

I know and the dead won't answer
if I'm not brave enough to speak it.

Terra Nullis

by day, I paddle
along the North Shore
towards Michilimackinac,
the homeland.

it's where I began,
under pine lined shores
in half sand, half scrub dunes,
before the Jesuits.

I went back as a child,
family outing in a green van,
posed in the garrison,
saw cannon fire.

it's lost to us now,
annexed by the army in 1815,
but the current runs North
and I follow.

when night finds me,
muscles torn, blisters on palms,
alone in a polyurethane tent,
cicadas haunt me.

the passage brings me
along the heart's inner value
to Lake Superior's chest,
but my lover isn't here.

he isn't anywhere,
terra nullis of the body,
but memory lives on,
it lulls the water.

if I reach Michigan,
retrace my ancestors exile,
I won't be over it: our divorce,
the genocide, my hydro bill.

with each stroke raised,
night storms on the water,
the splinters in my bones–
I mark what can't be lost.

this waterway route,
my instinctual drive to nest
in the inlet of the horizon,
the empty, the open, the wild,

Difficult

I'll say what I want.
this passage is difficult,
and I'm afraid.

I would go home,
if it existed, if I wasn't trans
and abandoned by God.

I'd call my friends,
if I could explain want.
only the land gets me.

I wish it was Christmas,
I need twinkle lights
and excuses to drink.

too many cigarettes,
I regret the lung ache,
but I crave company.

I won't follow straight men
on Facebook, Instagram,
or Youtube. I swear it.

when night comes,
I won't jump from cliffs
or disappear in dark water.

I will go on,
this is what I wanted,
freedom and choices.

but I will say everything
that crosses my mind,
my dreams taste of cedar.

this passage belongs to me-
unceded land, my sovereignty
carries me somewhere.

it isn't the home I deserve
but it is my only country,
wherever I land.

Lake Water

along the shoreline,
water waits in evening light,
a weight in the world
that holds the dark
as I do my coat,
close knit, cold.

the lake is immense,
gathered by time, rainfall,
the distant passage of glaciers
to rest against the Northern sky,
though I know it moves,
from Hudson's Bay to Superior.

at night, it's oppressive
beside me like a stranger,
alien and sovereign and secret,
gives life in one muted hand:
fish, mussels, wild rice.

the other offers death,
drowning, snakebite, the rapids,
so I'm uncertain what to say
tonight or tomorrow morning
when I greet it as I pass through
on my journey home.

I remember a poet saying
that water carries sound,
as if it knows how to amplify
the movement of all living things,
as if it knows how to speak
the mottled tongues of the dead.

this doesn't comfort me:
alone, my entire existence
about this single element.
my lungs are permeable
and I'm a bad swimmer,
I put tobacco down.

pray for water's mercy,
may the river run to source
so I can travel safe
across the glacial floodplain
to land on another shore,
but I don't believe in kindness.

I know enough of drowning
to see that only fire kills,
oxygen starved cells burning
in the lining of your veins.
water is just the absence
of air. It's nothing by itself,

but departure and suspension,
a portal to a world unknown
by human hands, a repository
of our discarded offerings:
plastic bottles, war ships,
lost ore from the mines.

this is small comfort to me,
knowing the water offers me
whatever I bring to it;
a sleeping bag, knapsack,
my old grief as ballast,
and it takes no more

than the weight of me,
moving by dawn over lakes
in a canoe, timid but certain
to be fixed on North like a compass,
as far from the earth and sky
as time can carry me.

Mollusk

when I sleep,
I dream in shadow.

the weight of water is my sky.

deep ribbons of blackness,
currents of starlight falter,
give way to the lake's roll,

my back curls
against the shore-bed
beside the husks of eels.

in my eye sockets,
quicksilvers circle as flesh jellies,
crayfish nest in my skull.

I am half awake,
unconscious but listing,
ribs turn starboard.

feet point west
against the breakers.
my bones are flint, sparking.

I will awaken
to rise with the lake tide,
deep enough to hold moonlight.

when I speak,
branded by the tongues of otters,
I say nothing of the night.

it's my promise,
an oath to the land,
to bear my wrecking with a certain grace.

not the grace of trees,
the smooth breasted laughter of bluejays,
but the grace of mollusks:

bottom feeder, black rimmed,
sharp under foot, slit mouthed,
small and as inescapable

as hunger.

What's Wild is Wild

I will not come this way again,
no second chances,
all regrets linger.

there is no fabled land,
no golden rivers shot through with light
and salmon. just black flies.

no cheers await me,
no one heralds my arrival
but a disinterested crane.

birds fly north, I wallow
in the rapids, drift in estuaries.
this vessel will be my tomb.

a rock face is unreadable,
I know that now, too late
to save my lips from frostbite.

what's wild is wild still,
I conquer nothing but my life,
death is my consolation.

being brave is not enough,
this backwoods suffers fools,
they disappear.

my quick mind
is as useful as my tongue,
there's no one to listen.

even the fish mock me,
white bones in my esophagus,
a hurt I can't spit out.

when I shit, it's blood.
poison ivy lines my bed,
my skin blisters, tears open.

I am alone, lost
in the hinterland beneath lichen.
every night I hear voices.

they call my name
between the dusk to dawn,
stone song slithers.

soon I will join them,
capsize in a slow topple,
ram the rapids with my spine.

when I die in this place,
a warning lesson to other idiots,
they'll air lift my corpse home.

I imagine it, my body lifting,
my skin inked by water's glint,
eyes tongued out by minnows.

the comfort of death's precognition,
to know that even if I fail,
if I don't make landfall,

if all paths lead to nothing,
there will be a homecoming.
if not for me as me, still

someone, somewhere,
will look for me and
I will be found.

Half Breed

not a mythic voyage,
just uncertain discovery,
casting out into a loon lit pond.

night insects, not compass points.

It's dark in the marsh,
I can't remember
how I got here.

inhale the bruised sky
pray with cigarettes
and wait for prophecy.

no one comes and it's cold.

my emptiness is pre-ordained.
the ancestors have nothing
to feed me, only scraps.

my fault so I load up,
head north from the city,
ghost ship in weekend traffic.

clueless halfbreed, exiled again.

I drove until the tank ran out,
portaged the Great Lakes
to this estuary, a mucking ground.

hungry with no offerings,
silent in the ancestral backwoods.
I blame my inheritance.

victimized by heritage, I admit it.

blood memory is genetic suffering–
residential schools and smallpox–
racism lingers, a colonial taint.

I'm hardwired for leaving,
true magnetic north is my sacrum,
Métis means transient, landless.

no treaties for half-breeds, just regret.

conquest isn't legendary to me,
descendant of exploration's tailings,
victim and rapist in one soul.

a spur in the spine, calcium trace
of an inland route on my ribcage
brings me to witness this marsh.

I have nothing, empty hands.

through the black, a bird calls out.
I wonder why I've come
but I see movement on the water,

hear a paddle on current,
smell tobacco- time slips
free to move towards me.

it's not a vision but memory

their journey from post to post,
hearth and kin tied to backs,
muscles tight, faces upturned–

they sing in Michif and English–

longing translates for me,
transient, alone with no record
but tendon's burn

but in us, the Great Lakes echo.

free along the shore,
no king nor country, just this land
and sound of our passage.

LAKE HURON

Lake Huron

half hour drive
from my home,

by the town of Goderich
before the tornado

tore up the lakefront,
sunk the salt mine cranes.

we came in summer,
winter and spring,

every season since my birth
to the artificial rock beach

my sisters, my mother,
once or twice my brother

brought us when
he learned to drive.

saw Canada Day fireworks
above the dune line,

found my first fish corpse
in the shallow inlets,

I haven't been back
since I left home,

distance too great,
I don't drive

what's left is memory,
the feel of lake water

when it's almost June,
not quite warm, cold

still holding winter,
a blue lightness

took my breath
from child sized lungs.

now I try to breathe
your gelatinous body,

how your water held me
in soft suspension,

whenever I feel like
dying.

Gills

I will not speak your names,
not on an emergency contact list,
the next of kin admission form,
not anywhere.

you are as blank as winter sky,
faded like the scar on my skin,
disappearance filed as suspicious,
an X file.

it is our shared punishment,
your absence and my silence,
the guilty texts with no reply,
their decibels beating.

once you asked for forgiveness,
an offhand comment at Christmas,
as if acknowledgement reconciles,
like admitting it matters.

I know what happened,
the things you meant to say,
doors forced open in the night,
welts across my spine.

you hit me for as long as I can remember
with whatever was at hand, each time
a different hurt, a new kind of bruise
to keep me in my place.

you said I disgusted you,
fat in sweatpants and always reading,
never wrestling with my brother
or catching the baseballs you threw.

you burned my lips once
with hair dye, an angry red line
that crusted over, bled all night,
I can't even remember why.

I still hear your voice,
asking me not to cry out,
don't make noise during,
no tears.

everyone thinks,
it wasn't that bad
and can't be true,
not really.

I don't mind the doubt,
feel the same hesitation
until a memory returns,
my grief flowers.

I remember ears ringing,
your hands on my skull,
dreams of murdering you,
my childhood in moments.

the price only I pay
while you deny it,
you remember nothing
so everything is mine.

the names I don't speak,
your faces in the car's front seats,
us laughing down highways,
the sweet remains.

all the violence,
like you made me
swallow a live fish,
twisting, sharp gills.

I don't speak to you,
I won't live you twice,
I know I can't leave you,
though I still try.

Photographs:
An Auto-biography

Age 0
small body, a black clump of hair,
huge blue eyes, your strongest feature
in your oversized head, wearing
a palm tree onesie.

impossible to imagine, yet
there's photographic evidence
of your beginning, a smile
on your baby face.

I keep a copy in a drawer
but never look, when I do
your eyes follow me,
asking to be saved.

you won't be saved,
smile or no smile,
this is as good as
it ever gets.

Age 8
a church photograph–
you look like yourself:
big nose, gay eyes.

it's before you got fat
but you can see it starting,
violence crowds the corner
of the lens.

the photo is banished,
it sat on your mom's dresser
through the beatings,
mocking you.

when you see it now,
you want to call the cops,
back in time and ask them
to lock up your father.

you want to find him,
the camera's captured boy,
send him to Toronto,
hideout on Church street.

but you know you can't help
even if the cops cared
and time was fluid
or destiny negotiable.

the photo lays it bare:
some kid, forehead too large,
who'll never be pretty
who will be brave but not enough

to put his photo up.

Age 14
gay as satan, like turpentine
burning in a glass jar,
a stereotype in fringe.

she's miming, blowing kisses—
prancing for the camera,
one hand lavish.

she's 14, a high school play,
a second suicide attempt
just days before.

the hospital released her
so she could perform,
no one knows.

they don't know
about the suffocation,
bags on her head

the cycle of eating,
vomit, starve, lose control–
repeat till her knuckles bleed.

when the photo ends,
when the play is finished,
she'll try again.

she won't ever stop,
not really, one form of it
her whole life.

the poems about death,
a terrifying nothingness
she bandies with.

it's on display,
her soul on fire,
lit up, choking.

she keeps the photo,
not for her condo walls,
but so she can mourn

everything she tried to kill.

Age 26

fat as you could get,
long hair, the worst plaid
with Christie Pits in foreground,
your author photo sweats.

it's accomplishment,
a photo for book jackets
taken by your lover's friend
on a grey Sunday.

you have everything here,
a partner and a house,
some friends, a book–
your body full with it.

Lake Huron

it's your eyes that make it,
bold and certain, as if
they'd finally struck gold,
learned to pierce suffering.

it's an embarrassment now,
80 pounds less, short hair,
boy gone back to Calgary,
you're nothing of what you were.

you get another done
if there was going to be
a second book, another life,
but you're not ready.

the photo on the jacket isn't you,
not anymore, you know
that's why you like it, because
it's all that's left of how it felt,

finally somewhere with someone
and something you wanted,
your eyes bright, as if loss
had never seen you.

Different

blue room, two windows–
one opened to the street,
the other to the yard.

at night I left them open
to hear the dogs bark,
trucks go by the house.

my sisters in the other room,
parents downstairs by the furnace,
their windows locked.

this is how I knew
my difference, even in sleep
I reached out

to dream of traffic
by water, the midnight haul
of life across the river.

Stalker

before I had a television,
I used to ride my bike
around the block for hours.

I wasn't allowed to read
those satanic books in the library
or see movies or listen to the radio.

so I biked, the pre-approved route
around my house, by the church,
across the dairy to the funeral home.

my favourite time was early evening,
just before darkness came to town,
when the lights clicked on in every window.

I used to watch them, the neighbours,
I didn't know their names or anything
but I liked their living rooms.

they would parade around, eating or talking,
televisions glowing and everyone so loud
I heard their conversations from the street.

sometimes I imagined living in those houses
but most of the time, I just kept my eyes
glued to their movements, like living museums.

no one knew, I was too young to matter,
and my parents never asked why I rode,
I never meant any harm, no malice in looking,

just wanted to see what it was like to have money
and not spend my days praying, repenting, hating.
it used to fuck me up, like I wasn't really alive.

as if my whole existence was a fraud
and everyone I saw in the neighborhood
were the real people, the ones who mattered.

I tried to stop but I missed the hunt for life
in the alleyways and side streets of town,
alone but a part of a hundred families,

every story mine, even if my only character
was witness.

Teeth

his hands wave above me,
spit flies from his mouth,
his words blister
and weep.

he's angry with me again,
for taking too long in line
for not showing respect,
for being.

I'm not sure how it begins,
a lurch in my spine
and I dart forward,
snap my teeth.

it doesn't break skin,
just leaves a red mark
where I bit him,
a shiny circle.

when he backhands me,
I lift up and drop.
a child on the floor,
breath gone.

the first time I bit a man,
my father at school,
but not the last time
I said no

with my teeth.

Swing Set

bent over, legs bare
and ass shaking,
I wait for pain,

like the swings
in the playground
wait for other kids

to start the rhythm
of falling and rising,
like I will when

he comes inside,
the maple board
in his hands,

the same smile
he wore to church
last Sunday.

Problem

they say I'm a troublemaker,
a problem child in the night,
who never stays quiet
or keeps to safe waters.

the same bullshit they said
·to my family, goddamn half-breeds
on the edge of Indian, squatters
and miscreants, reserveless.

I'm a nuisance in the blood,
the one who came back
and didn't waver, insisting
this land is still mine.

it's not only the mixed,
bleached out skin and blue eyes,
a sibilant lisp in my voice
and a sway in my hips.

faggot, fucking transsexual
in leather heels, lit up
laughing at the bar
like the fur queen I am.

I'm nothing they want,
smart and femme
without a pretty face
but a sharp tongue.

too much, too little of everything,
a descendant of a people
who were denied treaty
but kept our dignity.

they're half right, half honest–
I am in trouble, waist deep
in Canada's determined neglect,
the colonial predation of men.

they forget the violence
isn't my crime to answer,
no graves in my backyard,
no excuses on my cocksucking lips.

yes, I like white boys
and I can skin a bear
in more ways than one,
but no, I'm not anything

they say I am.

Waking

I dream of the old house,
dusk on the pines, fireflies glinting
through the low brush, and birds–
I can't say what kind- calling out,
the last noise of the day.

it's late summer in the dream,
I know by the earth's heat,
the banked sunlight diffusing
beneath my feet but faded,
maybe August, frost in the air.

across the dark, the tree line
waits for me, low and steeped
in shadow, a shaded green
by the yard's end, the footpath
to the river visible but only just.

I think I hear my mother,
not speaking but somehow a sound
of her in in the wind, an echo I
haven't heard in years but recall
and I'm scared to find her.

I stand at the bottom of hill,
beneath the house in the yard
and watch for explanations, signs
or omens to arrive, justify dreaming,
but there's nothing more:

just late summer, my old home,
the land slipping from light,
and my mother, lost to me,
but still singing with the birds,
the last sounds I hear

before waking.

Cold River

sing that cold water
I know so well,
be that dark current
I carry in my veins.

let it take me under
to the shallows in winter,
see the ice stretch above
an opaque and cracked sky.

listen for sturgeons
and feel the eels,
dream in hibernation
on the lakebed.

sing the winter water
I've been promised,
be that killing cold
I was born in.

wait for my mother,
count the dead here,
my gookum, my uncle,
everyone I knew.

forget the sun
I lied to,
give up the warmth
I wasted away,

sing that ice road,
pray for frostbite,
beg for winter's mercy,
be numbed by snow.

when spring comes
I'll be holy,
when summer comes,
I'll be transparent.

sing that cold water
my ancestor's grief,
all those bodies lost,
answer the drowned.

Wingham

far away from home now,
living in the city visited
only a couple of times:
baseball games, a wedding.

gone from dirt roads,
those musky farmhouses
and the smell of sheep shit,
folks in coveralls.

country music, the car show
the annual traveling circus,
pieces of my life gone
like water, never to return.

I miss parts of it,
the red brick town stores
lined up along Main Street,
foundry smoke in fall.

this is what happens to fags
in small towns and country counties–
I grew up and was forced out,
fled to the city.

some part of me,
a judgemental and wary side,
still lives there in a house
up the hill by the hospital.

I left the town
because I had no choice
but the town hasn't left me–
it's in me now.

one day, if only by death,
I'll go back and no one
will dare call me anything
but home.

The Business of Trauma

a friend tells me,
in passing, as if it's nothing,
she doesn't understand
all this business about trauma.

sure, she says, bad things happen
but I just think about all I have,
the money, the kids, the husband,
and it doesn't matter.

she adds, at least to me,
like an it's indictment,
as if I should know better
than to still hold hurt.

I think but don't say
grief has many names
but everyone negotiates it:
deny, celebrate, it's the same.

it's still your cross to bear,
whether to run from it
or say you're over it,
ignore the ice cracking.

I'll admit I've changed,
money means safety.
I like nice things,
those designer jeans.

if I could choose,
if the weight of loss
didn't keep me up,
the endless cataloging,

I'd trade it in,
a small and worthy life,
for a year of knowing
how to breathe again

not remember hands
around my neck,
my stinging thighs
crying into pillows.

it's nice to be happy
or at least fake it well
but what of ghosts,
what of me, age 6?

don't I deserve more
than compensation,
what of memory's promise,
can I mourn the unspoken?

I didn't reply,
let her words hang
so she could read assent
or disapproval, whatever.

it's not worth
explaining myself,
all victim impact statements
boil down to prove it.

I mourn the necessary,
because I had worth
and didn't deserve it,
I am a beautiful child.

it's not about overcoming,
that bit is done, I'm free.
now it's how to witness,
be honest with the dead

say they hurt me,
I'm not the same
since it happened,
I ask why.

yes I'm ok,
yes we're all ok.
sometimes the business
of trauma is a business.

it doesn't mean
you're wrong to struggle
with history, your story
is about what you lost

and what you've found.
saying it doesn't matter
is as useful as saying
it didn't happen at all.

sooner or later,
you have to fess up
and count the holes
in everything,

if not for yourself
then for everyone after
and everyone before:
this is what survival means.

a gift and a curse
to be the last one left,
at fault for nothing
but responsible for all.

I don't know much
of the business of trauma
I do know something
about loss,

enough to say
it matters to me
and I promise
it always will.

Rescue

growing up, I dreamed
of rescue.

crossing the border,
I used to pretend

I was kidnapped,
look distressed

and hope the guards
would notice, save me.

no one ever did,
not social workers

my aunts and uncle,
not my grandmother.

the people at church
or the postal office worker,

my teachers at school,
the boy in math class.

everyone looked right
past me, just another

distressed ember
outside the firepit

burning a hole
in the blanket

of town,
a problem

to be snuffed out
in time's forgetting.

I dream now
of retribution,

when the day
all the children

like me, the ones
with broken arms

and cut lips,
the starved

in basements
and shuffling

through hallways
like viruses

in the blood
of the happy

and white families,
the kids who

don't know when
it will end

and the ones
I know who jumped

or slit or hung
or just got high,

when I stop
waiting for the world

to find me and bring
my body home,

when I come
to the heart of it

with fists of prayers
and turn over graves,

storm every border crossing
demand to be seen

when I build a monument
to the missing and gone

in the middle of Walmart,
make the TV ads

show me hiding
from my parents

on Christmas,
when I force

everyone to admit
their joy is made

of my loss,
my body

something taken
as a price

for their safety
by predators

they didn't prosecute,
refused to name.

when I ask
for what I want,

for what hurt me most,
worse than being hit

or touched or choked,
the nothingness of abuse–

when I ask
to be seen

and everyone can't,
I don't let them,

look away, my face
shiny like a bruise

before it disappears,
when I come back

and open the doors
to light, the winter air;

that brief illumination
of my damaged selves,

this is the moment
I dream of now,

which isn't vengeance
nor redemption, nor rescue

just returning
to what I lost,

the sovereignty of truth,
of saying it happened

the universe admitting
it let me down and here

I am, not whole
but yes, still here

ready and willing
to be seen.

LAKE ONTARIO

Lake Ontario

you and me,
24 and 26,
the city behind us
with Lake Ontario
in spring light.

a rare Sunday,
restless in our skin
we walk to water,
you let me hold
your hand.

3 years together,
with 2 years left,
we know nothing.
love's retreat as
new as it's arrival.

as night appears,
our naivety is air,
it lifts us along
beside the lake
to the power plant.

we walk on through
residential neighborhoods,
kids call out, dogs
bark as we traverse
the city home.

we buy gelato,
eat it on my bed
by the front window
so we see dusk
through vanilla eyes.

you hold me
or I hold you,
we aren't sure
who is comfort,
who is angst.

we go to bed,
but wake all night
to fall asleep again
as if we sleep on waves
against the shoreline,

the constant weight
of rivers around us,
the night air escaping,
our bodies warm
as the possibility of love,

its ridiculous posturing,
evaporates into sunlight
when morning finds us
as the colour of blood
crowns over a lake

we won't visit twice.

December 11th

today is your birthday,
three weeks before Christmas.

every year we were together
I forgot it.

when we did insurance forms
or my passport application,

I had to text you to confirm
it really was December 11th.

I didn't forget this year,
your absence makes it easy.

which is the strange part of love,
how proximity deadens nerves

that departure reconnects
as constellations of neural ties.

a network of cellular hurt,
a distilled light in grey matter.

it's useful now, to remember
when you began in Calgary,

the same hospital you took me
when my wisdom teeth came in.

on Christmas eve, filled with drugs,
you walked me along the Bow River

while we waited for your dad
to drive us back home.

it's all connected, a loop
to snare every day in, a hook

of you in all the world,
just in my head, but still

happy birthday to you
in your parent's white house

surrounded by chocolate cake,
your sister's grainy Skype call

some sparkling white wine
in your mother's hand, your father's beer–

they're celebrating your 26th,
one year without me,

the first birthday I've missed
since you were 21 but there's that loop,

as if it matters what the calendar says
or when you began in this world:

what matters is when you began in me
and how you repeat in my cells,

that's the hook, love's return
is brain cells dying, I know

another boy's green eyes
will grow new ones

to form another galaxy
to fall back on, another date

to remember and keep fixed,
but I can't imagine love

as anything but your scent,
as if your stupid life was DNA

injected into my coronas,
reworking the inner circumference

today is your birthday
but every day since you left

gives birth to a new way
to miss you and our life

I still love you in my mind
like I love my dead dog

why you won't answer me
is as clear and certain as decay,

it's that loop, that hook
in love you can't get over

biology wins all,
what your mind avoids

only becomes stronger,
and that knot in you,

1 year old,
is me.

#Merrygrief

the wind tells me
it's almost Christmas,
as if lights aren't enough
to remind me.

I put up a tree,
the one thing I saved
during the divorce,
pre-lit and dusty.

I bought ornaments,
red, green, gold glass,
and the odd pieces
that don't belong.

what I won't do
is admit how much
it hurts every year
to face my emptiness.

another year wasted
on movement, on people
and still I'm alone,
wrapping gifts for one.

I will fill the tree–
I've escaped poverty
if not my childhood–
but no one will know.

as Christmas comes,
a countdown of days
with a strange urgency,
I measure my loss:

a family, four homes,
one lover, one dog,
too many friends,
the smell of woodsmoke.

on my way home,
a week before Christmas eve,
I see an ad asking for
my instagram Christmas wish.

I want to photograph
my stuffed tree, gift laden,
hashtag it merrygrief, wish
for a world I can't know:

one where good intentions
line my parka like prayers,
and that dark wind, cold nosed,
doesn't remind me of anything at all.

New Years Eve

I won't come home tonight,
along Yonge street, snowfall
covers the tracks of my escape.

the city lights are blue, red
in the white noise of winter,
but I look up to heaven.

it's colder now, January
spreads in the currents
of exhausts and cigarettes.

I don't notice windchill
or freezing point, just movement
past me on the sidewalk.

everyone is heading back
to source, their warm dens
and the tv's distant light.

all the things I know
are somewhere else,
I got left behind.

alone, almost 30,
another calendar year turning
around my empty mouth

the winter is mine,
a certain point of loss
accumulating in my centre

like snowfall on Lakeshore,
city plows rushing to meet
a continuous and infinite adversary.

so it's fair to say,
to the intersection of Wellesley
at 4 am on New Years Eve

I won't be coming home
tonight or any night I know,
even if I go back

to Wingham, to London
to Little Italy or Davenport,
someone new lives there now

like this late season storm,
it's freezing rain and winds,
I am destined to arrive

where everyone is leaving
and swirl, discordant in the dark,
past the edges of their eyes.

Trillium

the animal in me
is constant.

thirst starts,
hunger answers.

sleep is uncertain,
restless limbs.

in the night,
I hear footsteps.

warnings appear,
all signs say death.

still I crave
cigarettes, coffee.

exhaustion brings
repetition, life cycles.

cold follows me,
something waits.

telegraphs move faster
than my heart.

I stay primitive,
gestate in trilliums.

when the hunter
finds me, separate

I turn toward the blow,
bleat into sacrifice.

domesticated prey,
still wild enough to leap

against my instinct,
find my predatory drive

and tear the throat out
of what chases me.

Second Hand

I feel it in my lungs,
a tightness from smoking
or my infinite desire.

I am going towards death,
it's real to me now
as it never was before.

there's a certain arc
to my descent–
soon I disappear.

the tightness predicts
the likely culprits,
cancer, AIDS,

or a violent encounter.
All the gifts I know
girls like me receive.

when I dream
it's corrupted
by city scenes

where I run from
moving corpses
into cold rivers.

it's not angst,
the kind of worry
children have

when a relative dies,
I'm not afraid
but hesitant to leave.

like at parties,
when I walk in,
hungry eyes asking

if this is my moment
and it isn't so I linger,
strain for some good.

it's the reaching
which kills me,
why the tightness aches

more than it should,
sends me over the edge
to full blown panic.

I want her,
the girl no one sees,
to catch something more

than infection or tumours,
pray for a second coming
worthy of her.

I laugh it off,
breathe the constriction
like I've mastered it,

ignoring the days
that fall around me,
spent with nothing left.

my lungs blacken,
bones fix and age,
I am receding

as the river looms,
no one will find me
tonight, not ever–

and it's me,
the same as ever,
smoking in the stairwell

I want to stop
but I turn to face
the second hand light

to head for home,
though I doubt
I will make it back alive,

I can't help smiling
because I know
I still try.

Warp

the last time,
our old house
empty of our things,
floorboards bare
and the radiators
silent at last.

you asked me
to help pack
what was left,
your brother-in-law
and best friend
as awkward witness.

you said nothing
out of the ordinary,
just hello, goodbye
as the truck drove
away on Avenue,
and I closed up.

this is our end,
your face in light,
a May 1st move,
me smoking on
the back steps,
five years gone.

and our house,
now someone else's,
blessed by my hands
along the railing,
against the doorframes,
a silent offering.

what could you say,
I know, it's not fair
to expect more of us
than a soft landing.
we never fought
or said mean things.

we laughed at others,
the crazy couples,
your friend's rough sex,
pregnancy scares,
miscarriages, weddings,
ex lovers sleeping over.

I told you
we were better,
because I thought
we loved enough
to hold tongues,
keep the peace.

now I wonder,
our last time
in the front room,
you standing there
with your hands full
of our life, the kitchen table.

if I missed the mark
of telling you the truth
about love, how you
used to rest in me
like a warp in the floor,
the tilt in our house

sending things rolling
to the centre of it
as shifting foundations
made ceiling cracks,
how we joked we
had to break up

before the house did,
the walls failing as

everything went south,
the gravity of us
pulling me home,
we tried to hold fast.

you said nothing either,
stiff lipped camaraderie
like an old bar friend,
as if we never fucked
leaving with the furniture
so I had to lock

our door forever,
words in my mouth.
you, flying back
to Calgary, your life
in June's transient heat,
never revealing yes,

this was our home.
love lived here, even if
we didn't learn it's scientific name,
even if we weren't certain,
even if we parted without
saying thanks.

Nightfall

no one looks for me by nightfall,
I make camp but does it count
if the only witness is a murder of crows,
laughing in their spruce houses.

I used to dream of aloneness,
back when the divorce wasn't sure
and I spent every night shifting,
his sleeping body beside me.

this quiet dark is not busy,
solitary lines of shadow grow
but they don't hold me.
still it's not peace.

distance looms in the space
between the sky and my flashlight,
the small circle of my tent
as full of longing as our old house.

how funny the heart is,
an animal in me that wants
whatever the wind brings it,
to hunt, nest, or die.

but tonight I know different,
count the stars, an infinite sprawl
that seems to span the Great Lakes
in cold light, a marker of how far

I've come from him
and how close to me
he remains.

LAKE ERIE

Lake Erie

I'm the girl
who saw light
through your
empty waters.

legally dead
in the 80s,
jacked up
on runoff,

fertilizer made
algae blooms
and closed
your beach.

you resurrected,
fish swam home
as streamers
of green awoke.

now you grow
verdant again,
the smallest lake
with the most tourists.

I've changed too,
no longer a child–
a woman with
blue eyes.

we meet again
in high summer,
two daughters
of rainfall,

everyone said
we couldn't be
saved, never
whole again.

but the wonder
of a girl in a lake
is a promise,
we come back

even if no one
can believe
we still know
how to swim.

Fuck Me

my friend tells me,
between pull ups,
women don't say
what we want

the patriarchy
trains us to be
afraid of desire,
as if we're tinder

in a heavy downpour
undercover by the lake,
too elemental to spark
even in careful hands.

I think she's right
even if we sound like
the women's studies
majors we are.

she asks me
to write out
what I want,
if I'm comfortable

confessing my desire,
describing my sex
without science words
or a diagram.

I try and end up
with garbage,
useless metaphors
about constellations.

the next time we meet,
I say all I want
is a man who
listens.

Kensington Series

for Wes

A:

I imagine the inside
of your t-shirt,

the space between
fabric and chest hair,
your heartbeat.

what I want is
to pass my hand
along the seam

of your public body
and it's hidden twin,
the underself

of your skin,
the part of you

no one knows,
except for night air

this want
is the closest

I come
to prayer.

B:

I want the impossible,
to be the kind of girl
boys like you desire

not just for experimental sex,
late night encounters hidden
from the real girlfriends

the ones you introduce
to parents and call beautiful,
the girls I see on the street

in their short dresses, hairless
with their hands in your hands,
no one looking or evaluating

whether they pass judgement
if their walk is feminine enough,
no one asking if they are worthy

I know they suffer as well
from your masculinity,
the power you posses

from a distance, the price
of femininity seems worth it,
to have your admiration

and carry life in my body,
wear my skin without thinking
today might be the day I end up

in a garbage bag by the Don Valley,
checking my shoes to make sure
I can run fast enough to get away.

so ask me again in your voice,
your eyes meeting mine, hands
seconds away from touching

what my life is about,
I'll tell you I'm a priestess,
summoning joy from a darkness

only I see.

Lake Erie

C:

I want a boy
like you, who isn't afraid
to step across the lines

of the bodies we are
allowed to desire.

I want a boy
like you, who isn't afraid
to trace the line of my neck

as if I'm an ice road about
to crack.

I want a boy
like you, who wants a girl
like me even if I don't pass,

even if the love I have
is one without a name.

I want a boy
like you, but I know
boys like you can't want

girls like me, even if we're
the ones who want your love

most.

Fake It

bad sex, the same boys
I always fuck.

they love my dick
despite my indifference,

even though I can't fake
masculinity or dominance.

I keep trying, determined
to overcome biology.

somehow it betrays,
the woman I am

wants to stroke their hair,
tell them it's good.

comfort their small worries
or bake a pie, not fuck.

I believe in female desire,
that women can screw,

be avaricious gods,
do pegging, things with whips.

but not my femininity,
that old bush wife nurturing

who needs game to skin,
wants to give sinew purpose.

I need a practical man
who understands sex

is a kind of creation,
a duality of purpose

and what I bring
is soft and certain,

the lake in April, thawed,
banked in green

not a line of hardness,
to parade around, to show off

everything my cock is
is everything I'm not,

their disappointed faces
remind me of how far my body is

from who I want to be.

Fucked

I won't be fucked,
not because of pain
though it still half hurts,
an inner resistance
that never goes away.

I won't be fucked,
not by that high school friend
who married too young
and drunk texts me,
looking for sympathy.

I won't be fucked,
not by the boys at the bar
strangers on the waterfront,
hipsters on the subway,
or the Starbucks barista.

I won't be fucked,
like my gookum was
by a man I hate
whose kids I've borne,
whose money I need.

I won't be fucked
like my mother's daughter
in the bedroom,
polite and childlike,
confused by consequences.

I won't be fucked
by anyone anymore,
worn out and bored
by repetition, blood loss,
the aching in my eyes.

I won't be fucked,
as stupid as is it is
to reason with desire,
negotiate surrender,
save myself like rain water.

Trout

it's my birthday,
28 years old and still afraid.

my friends got me drunk,
bought a lap dance in the village.

I should be euphoric,
he's 21, uncut, Russian.

heavy accent but slight shoulders,
both wary and persuasive.

in the backroom, he asks
what turns me on.

I answer "just normal",
meaning blank slate, desire mouthless.

Rihanna plays on speakers overhead,
he touches himself and me.

he moves in the half light
like an apparition.

I'm not hard but not soft,
caught between memory and muscle.

fleeing isn't an option,
my friends wait by the stage

so I let him grope me,
guide my face along his back.

he makes me hold him,
spreads my palms open,

my fingers on his hip bones,
it reminds me of baptism,

as if him and I are praying,
absolution in the darkness.

he turns and kisses my neck,
I tear up then hide it,

rest my face in his chest,
my lips on the collarbone's hollow.

he smells like deodorant,
sweat and shit,

he senses the shift,
the half full erection,

so he holds me, bobs
like a boat on slow water.

I wish my cock was braver,
certain in its presence,

because he's beautiful,
and I would fuck him

or be fucked by him,
I`m not sure which,

if I could close the distance
between me and the boys,

the ones who've reached me
and the one who raped me,

the dads who've beat me off,
and the dad who beat me,

I can't and the music stops,
lap dance over.

I apologize, look away,
he says he understands,

tells you his brother took him
to a strip club for the first time

he was 18 and remembers
what it's like to be nervous.

I tip him and leave
without explaining,

it's not nerves,
just mistranslation.

I only know desire
as a trout knows the shore,

in death, defeat,
and a fisher's lure.

Taking It

if I let a boy fuck me,
I find myself

inconsolable under him,
the pressure of his cock

inside me like a threat,
anxiety in waves as I

feel muscles contract,
my rectum expanding

to drive me along
my orgasm, confused

between pain and the fear
of rupture or infection,

being fucked feels fatal,
as if I could die

from his carelessness,
his rushed performance

as he seeks his pleasure
in the boundaries of me,

like my father with his belt
or boys at school chasing me,

as if he needs me to give up
and surrender, to let him in

to my interior, the hinterlands
of my heart, the wild

in me caught by his sex,
staked out in place, an offering

to my desire, I want
his love even if it hurts,

I come back to him
every time, asking it to be different

finding the same ache,
the blood in the toilet after,

but I feel some expansion
grow in my body during,

when I want him out
but can't say stop,

I'm hard, sunk on his cock
breathing through my skin

and I cum, hands free,
caught in wonder,

my voice cut up
as skin flushes pink,

I feel warmth like shitting
spread through my hips

and it's alright to be taken
and wronged once more,

to be let down by a man,
pushed to a complete loss

but saved from disaster,
brought back from the edge

not by his haphazard fucking,
but my body's instinctive drive,

its ability to call pleasure
and bring me water in drought,

its desperate and certain power
to carry weight in pelvic bones,

my prostrate like a diving bell,
ringing out the way back

to the light.

Self-Love

A:

I saw a night sky
in winter, just before
the sun slid away,
an infinite blue light
folded into dark
as cold called
from the North,

everything by me
stopped to watch
the movement of air,
as light on heaven
turned inward to gather
along the horizon
like smoke underwater.

the ordinary passage
of day to night, nothing
I would write home about
but so certain in its beauty,
so fixed in its revelation.
I never forgot the moment
when the light stopped

a sudden blackness
took the world over,
birds made no noise
the poplars were still
I breathed the night,
a complete offering
to a wonder I can't name

I still carry its grace,
see the dark beauty
of a clear winter night
filled with ancestors
over Georgian Bay
whenever I look in
my eyes.

B:

I remember
being a kid,
dressing up
like a girl
with friends

we paraded out
to our parents,
happy in line
in long skirts
and cheap lipstick.

my dad said
he felt sick
to his stomach,
seeing his son
looking like that

he kept saying
"imagine how I feel"
all the ride home,
everyone quiet
in the car but him.

as if he was cheated
by God and destiny
to father a boy
soft as his sisters,
who liked to dance.

I still remember
his eyes when I
walked into the room,
shirt on my waist
and a pink necklace

but I don't regret
a moment of life
on the other side
of my father's love,
a place I've learned

is the wide house
every woman builds
when a man shames her
and she decides her love is
the only love she will suffer for.

What I Want

what I want
is to be held

like the sky holds
lakewater, diffuse

and interspersed
with celestial bodies.

what I want
is the slow movement

of roots along the shoreline,
the drawing close of life

to what feeds it,
moisture in my lungs.

what I want
is a love like winter

a cold mountain, absolute
and still in the dark

of 5 am, a certain weight
to cover all my dreaming.

what I want
is a discovery of trees

in April's sudden warmth,
to bud at a glance,

my soft green lashes
threading in temporary wonder.

what I want
is a boy

who knows the Northern praises,
the memory of stones

in his hands, a rough callus
of grief behind his eyes,

who sees me coming
across the floodplain

and spreads his bones
to guide me home

along the North Shore
of my body,

what I want
is the promise

of a new land
in the ancestral arms

of every season
I am heir to.

LAKE SUPERIOR

Lake Superior

mother, I said every prayer
you taught me, every tongue
a flicker of ash, every word
a sedimentary insect.

I gathered light
in the fat cells of my belly,
a river-fed trout caught
in bent hooks, bloodied.

I was brave
in downstream aggregation,
insistent on the tenuous
rhythm of reeds.

I came twice
in summer's lakebed grit,
flat down and legs up,
sunk my desire.

I cut skin
on stinging nettles,
ate bulrush stems,
swam in muskgrass.

I had nothing
but your praises, the line
of me like a heron's dive
to blackwater, sharp.

I carried you
in my clavicle as a rockface
carries yesterday's rain,
your iodine skin glinting.

I waited long
in the corridor of aspen,
hunched my bones
by the cedar trails.

I've done all
the migratory birds asked,
left seeds along snowbanks,
made peace with cold.

I've lived
29 years in your watershed,
how long will it take me
to forget you?

I promised
to be honest, to stand
against the stars and
the moon's aura.

I admit
you brought things
to fill the lodge of me,
crayfish and myths.

I wish you
were less than
a lake beneath sky,
more than weight.

you are
fire and rivers,
you are nothing,
everything I know.

I loved
your split hands,
indulgent narrows,
and inlet spines,

I still love
your persistent depth
of 1,333 feet where
all water gathers.

I am student
to your mysteries.
in wonder of you, I learn
how to create life;

I know your tides
are not real, not by gravity
or the rotation of the earth,
you only mimic oceans.

this what you've taught me,
inferior daughter of glaciers–
alone in your rock shield,
in this land, we must mother

our illusionary grandeur,
not dishonest, this change
to become another deposit
of an infinite regurgitation

we call beauty, mother
you and I know it's just
a different name
for life.

Death

I wonder if immortals transition,
a vampire in heels at MAC,
looking for flawless coverage,
powder to soften cheekbones.

maybe it would be easy,
infinite opportunities to blend
and the best collection of corsets,
400 years of makeup practice.

if I ever meet a transgendered
vampire with genderless pronouns,
I'm going to compare notes,
offer up my mortal wisdom,

how aging pushes me out
into places I never meant to go,
how death makes me kind
and got me into heels

the first time, the last time,
every time I dared to become
was because of the knowledge
I might not wear this dress again.

Resolution

spend the day alone
counting the ways
I let myself down.

I haven't quit desire
even if it brings me
visions at night.

say how I broke
everything handed to me,
how I sunk ships

in the deep water,
how I left the dishes
piled in the sink.

I didn't grow
a thicker skin,
a new set of lungs.

I am the same,
the girl who ran south
along the highway

stopped for nothing
until she found the lake
and returned to every grief

she promised to forget.

Girls

I know it's possible,
to step from one body
to another, to be cut free
from biology, to cheat God,
be the woman I am.

I've heard the surgeons
describe the procedure,
counted the hormone pills,
watched facial feminization,
done the medical math.

two years of therapy,
two years of electrolysis,
one year of dilation,
a lifetime of risk:
cancer, complications.

I have the makeup,
can walk in heels,
speak in a higher voice,
a closet of dresses,
my favourite leather boots.

I've heard the odds,
recovery time, rejection,
explaining yourself at borders,
been chased down alleyways,
felt the way men stare.

I know everything I need to
about the physical, the danger
of it but nothing of the joy,
to see my face as it is
in daydreams–

to become her.

I can't say what's right
for the girls I know,
the ones like me,
in between and outside,
our dicks tucked in lace.

I could accept it,
the imperfect change
to a body still not mine,
no uterus, never passing,
burning my veins in chemicals.

if I knew the boy I seem
could melt away, step back
to let the girl I am in,
if I knew she just waited
for me to cross that river.

what stops me isn't fear,
of not being beautiful,
becoming a freak,
being more alone,
making a mistake–

but the burden of her desire,
how much she wants
from life, how much
she deserves. I can't
give anything less

than everything she ever
needed to be.

Trans

I'm like the lumberjack
in Monty Python,
the husky guy
with wide shoulders,
a heavy beard.

he wants to wear
women's clothing,
high heels, tights,
hang around in bars,
call boys "Hun".

just like me,
on weekends in leather,
second hand dresses
purple wig, bad makeup–
zero fucks, no date.

it's not enough,
dangerous roleplay
in tolerant clubs, 80s parties
with strangers who laugh,
pose for pictures.

it's the best we have,
the lumberjack and me,
a comedy show for straights,
jokes for guys, snickers–
daring to touch us.

but I like the feeling
of being mistaken
for a woman, the fun
of transformation,
my second life.

if it feels wrong,
like cheating myself
by not going far enough,
if it makes me sad
to wipe away my makeup,

at least it's funny
to someone, my body
stuffed into a form
it can't quite mimic,
my eyes luscious.

there's power
in admitting you aren't
the real deal, in facing
the crowd, the indifferent boys–
my calves tired, my face

radiant in the exhilaration
of reaching for myself,
in showing the truth
of my mascara heart,
nothing is more beautiful

than a woman who knows
exactly what she wants
and what I want
is myself.

Blue

first things first,
the blue is infinite.

it began in me
when I was born,

my first room,
my wide eyes.

the colour of sleep,
my animal circus comforter,

a roving skyline,
my town's default setting.

everything I know
is blue's imaginings.

not easy, not restful,
the colour of deep space.

winter's light to dusk,
bruises on my back,

melodious and searching,
a byproduct of distillation,

it is not real,
not like the rest.

arriving from abstraction,
an apparition of light,

it only reveals absence,
chance interplay of molecules.

this is why it exists
beyond my calculations

why I love it more
than the light or dark,

when I die, let it be
my incandescent shroud.

coat me in tap water,
open the windows to daybreak

watch the infinite blue
evaporate from me,

damp residue on a glass,
disappearing from sight

like frost on the tree line,
a passing shine on dullness.

everything the blue is,
temporary and unreadable.

you only see it
when it's leaving

you cannot follow
to blue's source,

heaven, an underground spring,
a galactic wreath of starlight.

it will return,
diffuse and changed

in another illuminated moment,
a new shadow on the floor.

the same for me,
my birth and death

begin and end with blue,
its transient shade.

so first things first
then last things last,

mourn me as you would
the colour of this present sky,

a blue light beyond you
fated to never appear

twice.

A Good Medicine Song

another day alone,
halfway to heaven
in a strange city,
home but not at peace.

I wonder about my life,
the groove of my mind
like a spring willow bank,
mud, roots and shoots.

I barter probabilities
like rough crows cawing
at the coming night,
tree top vigil on a flat horizon.

will I escape violence,
the kid in me kicks
at everything hard,
"back the fuck up" anger

worn thin at the edges
where dawn rubs in,
its tenacious light
bringing a rare calm

which doesn't soften me,
though the beauty tries
to soak the calluses
in empathic milk

I'd like to be gentle,
mellow the harshness
of my bones in lye,
melt to calcified jelly

be graceful in low brush,
deer stalking the infinite,
but I'm brash, trillium white
amidst the hidden green.

that's the way of abuse,
I guess, how it leaves you
walking down gravel roads
to empty spaces, your life

a map of graveyards,
battlefields where you died
and resurrection stones
upturned, I think

I'd like something to happen,
unlooked for and wondrous,
meteor showers in June,
a boy who stays.

but I can't count on it,
just this half life of days
across the revenant land,
boots wet, jeans dusted up

nothing before me,
everything behind,
my hands bare,
my soul a stone.

River

it's going to get me
sooner or later.

the price I paid
is a debt owed,

I'm not sure
who collects

the prayers of children,
their sudden pain

when their father
comes at night

to leave welts
along their skin.

I know
whoever holds the bill

has my name
written in bold

on a page
marked "destiny".

I've escaped
so many predators

by chance or rescue,
most often by

taking it better
than others could.

I didn't die
in that town,

even if I hung
myself twice

before 14,
even if they ran

after me with dogs,
left notes asking

me to suck cock
behind the swimming pool.

I made it to 20,
if the odds were low

because no one
taught me anything

I couldn't learn
from a boxing class,

even if Crohn's
made me shit blood

for weeks, endless
cramps, ER visits

with the scars
on my left hand

from the IV tracks,
I almost died

alone in a waiting room
begging for help.

I sought love,
from strangers and friends

boys I met online,
in bars and parks

risked AIDS,
a violent ending

every time I let
them fuck me

even if it reminds
me of rape,

of my father's hands
above my naked body,

even if I think
it's a regressive roleplay

from the deacon
touching me in the basement.

once I saw a handgun
resting on the shelf

above the bed,
bent over, thinking

this guy will kill me
if I don't give him

everything I am,
he didn't.

here I am,
28 years later

at my half life,
still smoking

in secret outings
behind the parking lots,

80 pounds less,
half starved, waiting

for my death
to find me,

writing poetry
to make strangers

think they have it better
to know beauty

from the inside out,
as if their deaths

will come any sweeter
than mine, as if they

can escape time
with love's opioid taste,

but I know,
even if I don't say

what's coming for me,
the promised suffering

I deserve it
my parents said

God finds me repulsive
sends his angels to kill

faggots in our wickedness
I asked for it,

the beatings
the names, the bottles

thrown at my head,
my vomit in the sink.

I've been lucky
to pass notice

for so long, luckier
than the other kids

I met in the hospital,
locked ward.

some jumped
bled out, or just starved,

I've outlived them
it's a small grace

to say I mattered
held to some place

the violence never found,
but the timid mercy of life

won't save me, won't
keep me back from it.

I was born to this,
this dark river is mine,

it's here, right now
in the spaces between

every word I write
every breath I take

only brings its waters
closer to my door.

Ceremony

may this poem
be a prayer

in the soft down
of evergreen beds

grown by Lake Superior
to shelter me.

may this poem
be vowels of water

so rivers lift me
through this land

on ancestral currents
to where I began.

may this poem
be an offering

to carry me
through this pain

to the North Shore
where my heart rests.

may this poem
be a promise

to the woman
who has slept

inside me for years
that her eyes are open.

may this poem
echo the voices

of my grandmothers
as they stand behind

the cover of stars
to hold me up.

may this poem
bless my body

as hormones warp it
and surgeons mark it

as it catches fire
to burn boy from girl.

may this poem
be a map to mark

the place I begin
as a woman,

which is not
between my legs.

may this poem
be a softness

to fall on my skin
and soak my bones

so I grasp the world
with nothing between me.

may this poem
carry me past

men on the street
who laugh or spit

to remind me my gender
is judged by their desire.

may this poem
answer every wrong

I have borne
and lift my family

to forgiveness in lodges
bound of cedar.

may this poem
be the love I want

in the long night
when fear finds me

and its words guard me
in the weight of truth.

may this poem
be the kindness of men

who read my skin
like a farmer's almanac

and speak my name
as a sovereign promise.

may this poem
last as long as

I live on this earth
and follow me

like my yellow dog
across every passage.

may this poem
remind me as often

as I forgot to honour
my second girlhood

how the water in me
is still mine.

may this poem
walk on the land

under blue sky
to water and swim

as a trout beside me
through shore beds home.

Passage

think of beauty, its varied form
moving towards you as if
bound to you as water
is bound beneath the sky.

think of the mountains in Banff,
snowfall with the first light
crossing the boundaries
of cloud cover.

think of midsummer Lake Huron,
French fry vendors, seagulls
in their endless cries, mother
reading, her face red.

think of the dog, brand new
in the green bathtub, first wash
across yellow fur, his legs
falter and shake.

think of whiteouts on roads,
coming from hockey to a farm,
temporarily one of the boys,
dad drives slow.

think of country churches,
high ceilings, the sound of hymns
as rainfall soaks sheep grazing,
caught in beauty.

think of Michigan, Cheeze-It crackers,
backwoods gravel roads,
Gookum's kitchen, aunties' gossip,
cigarette smoke circles.

think of laying in a birch lodge
fire keeping for fasters at 3 am,
a boy from Six Nations sleeps
beside you as the owls pray.

think of your sister singing,
the windows open to town,
air tongued with humidity,
her voice heavy with lilacs.

think of the highway by town,
full of transport trucks at night,
air brake orchestra for sleep,
the comfort of headlights.

think of a Calgary night broke open,
western sky as if darkness means
you're home, ghosts in windows,
wind on the reservoir.

think of the boy, first time you met
in the Kensington coffee shop,
cold rain, his white shirt damp,
your skin electric.

think of the earth, a million bodies
move outside your house,
each one made of familiar memories
arranged in new patterns;

think of the beauty you know
send it into the current, see it
return to a distant source
you cannot follow.

think the price of wonder
is grief but everything repeats,
even if it's lost, even if death
takes us again and again.

think we can't come twice
to the place beauty waits,
as soon as we arrive, it departs
to return changed.

think of the beauty you know,
imagine we never forgot:
the beauty we know
is only the passage to us.

Goes On

the passage is infinite
but I'm not.

I break down,
molecular divergence.

when I depart,
cigarettes butts linger.

ash streaks on granite,
where I've butted out

modern petroglyphs,
"this way comes longing."

my skin alternates,
first freeze then molten.

northern sunlight
washes my bones.

memory guides hands,
motion carries me.

when the day ends,
I disembark into nothing.

sleep under stars,
each bed is a new grave.

yes, it's endless,
the weight of grief.

this country knows
nothing else.

but it's easy to forget
along the river's arc,

that everything I've been
is everywhere I am.

the land goes on,
even if I can't.

Acknowledgements

To my dead, because we are still responsible to each other. To my physical and spiritual ancestors, Indigenous and Queer, because your stories carry me forward.

To Renee, Allison, and Kateri, for all of their support and work on this book. Special acknowledgement for Kegedonce's work to champion the voices of Two Spirited writers and for taking chances on experimental works like this.

To Kat V, for all of the amazing editorial work and insights. You are one of the most talented and generous poets in Canada today. You reflect the wonder and power of our people, which is the highest praise I know. Also thanks for teaching me about epitaphs.

To Ashley Emma, for an amazing headshot and being the coolest person ever.

To Shane R, for telling me that no one reads poetry anymore, so we can write whatever we want. To Jack Illingworth, for being a champion of Indigenous writing and writers.

To Glad Day Bookstore and everyone who volunteers/works to support/create diverse Queer literature in Toronto, esp. Michael and Scott.

To Cherie, Shaun, Janine, Sonam, Karen, David, Susan, Jan, Aaron, and Sarah for making this small life feel large (and for teaching me to use foundation and protecting me while I wander around Toronto in 5 inch heels).

To the boys on Instagram, because longing takes me where I need to go. This book wouldn't have been written without the motivation of your narcissistic selfies/confusing interior landscape shots. #desirestopchasingme #hipster #gay #beard #inked

To survivors, the ones here and the ones who aren't.

To girls like me. We're the rarest of Pokémon. #transisbeautiful

Most of all, thanks to myself for writing this book, because it wasn't easy. #darklady

I am extremely grateful to the support of the Ontario Arts Council and the Canada Council for the Arts who have provided funding to support the completion of this project.